Whiskey Business Secrets
Crafting Liquid Gold

Chapter 1
Introduction

Starting a Whiskey Business

Whiskey has long held a special place in the hearts of connoisseurs, a drink of contemplation, character, and craftsmanship. The allure of crafting and sharing this beloved spirit is a dream for many. However, starting a whiskey business is no small endeavor. It requires dedication, knowledge, and a deep appreciation for the art and science of whiskey-making. In this chapter, we will embark on the journey of exploring what it takes to establish and run a successful whiskey business.

Why Start a Whiskey Business?

The first step in any entrepreneurial venture is to understand why you're drawn to it. Whiskey has a rich history and an enduring appeal. Some of the key reasons for starting a whiskey business include:

1. Passion: If you have a genuine passion for whiskey and a desire to create exceptional spirits, this could be your calling.

2. Craftsmanship: Whiskey-making is a blend of art and science. Crafting your own unique whiskey can be deeply satisfying.

3. Tradition: Whiskey has a tradition that stretches back for centuries. You can become a part of that heritage.

4. Business Opportunity: The global whiskey market is substantial, and there is room for new players, innovative ideas, and unique flavors.

5. Community: The whiskey community is passionate and supportive. Building a business in this industry allows you to connect with like-minded individuals.

6. Legacy: Creating your brand of whiskey can be a legacy to pass on to future generations.

Market Overview

Before delving into the practical aspects of starting a whiskey business, it's crucial to understand the whiskey market. This includes recognizing key trends, consumer preferences, and the competitive landscape. Here are some important points to consider:

- Market Size: The whiskey market is substantial, with a global reach. The demand for quality whiskey continues to grow.

- Consumer Preferences: Consumers are increasingly interested in unique and craft whiskeys. Understanding what your target audience desires is vital.

- Competitive Landscape: Many well-established whiskey brands dominate the market. You'll need a solid strategy to stand out and compete effectively.

- Regulations: The whiskey industry is highly regulated. Complying with local and international laws is essential.

- Trends: Trends in whiskey, such as the rise of craft distilleries, flavored whiskeys, and sustainability, can influence your business decisions.

Starting a whiskey business is both an art and a science, and it demands a strategic approach. In the chapters that follow, we will delve deeper into the various aspects of this fascinating journey. Whether you're an aspiring distiller, a whiskey enthusiast, or a business-minded individual, this book will provide the knowledge and guidance to help you embark on your whiskey-making adventure. So, let's raise a glass to the possibilities that await you in the world of whiskey entrepreneurship.

Chapter 2
Whiskey Basics

Understanding the Heart of Whiskey

Whiskey, often referred to as "liquid gold," is a spirit that has captured the hearts and palates of enthusiasts for generations. To embark on a journey of starting a whiskey business, it's essential to begin with a solid understanding of the fundamentals. In this chapter, we will explore the basics of whiskey, from its origins to the intricate distillation process.

The Origins of Whiskey

The roots of whiskey are buried deep in history, and its creation is a testament to human innovation and resourcefulness. While it's difficult to pinpoint the exact birthplace of whiskey, it is widely believed to have originated in one of the Celtic nations, potentially Ireland or Scotland. The name "whiskey" itself is derived from the Irish term "uisce beatha" or "usquebaugh," which means "water of life."

Types of Whiskey

Whiskey comes in various styles and types, each with its own unique characteristics. The main types of whiskey include:

1. Scotch Whisky: Hailing from Scotland, Scotch whisky is known for its smoky and peaty flavors. It's often aged for several years in oak casks.

2. Irish Whiskey: Irish whiskey tends to be smoother and lighter in flavor than Scotch. It can be triple-distilled and comes in various styles, such as single malt and blended whiskey.

3. Bourbon: Bourbon is a distinctly American whiskey made primarily from corn. It's known for its sweet and full-bodied profile and is aged in new charred oak barrels.

4. Rye Whiskey: Rye whiskey is made from at least 51% rye grain and has a spicier and drier taste compared to bourbon.

5. Single Malt Whiskey: Single malt is made from 100% malted barley and is produced at a single distillery. It's known for its complex and rich flavors.

6. Blended Whiskey: Blended whiskey combines different malt and grain whiskies to achieve a specific flavor profile. It's a common style in Scotland and Ireland.

The Distillation Process

At the heart of whiskey-making is the distillation process, a carefully controlled transformation that turns raw ingredients into liquid gold. Here's a simplified overview of the steps involved:

1. Mashing: Grains, usually a combination of barley, corn, rye, or wheat, are ground into a coarse flour and mixed with hot water to create a mash. The enzymes in the grains convert starches into sugars.

2. Fermentation: Yeast is added to the mash, and fermentation begins. This process converts the sugars into alcohol, resulting in a liquid called "wash."

3. Distillation: The wash is heated in a still to separate alcohol from water. This produces a high-proof spirit known as "new make spirit."

4. Aging: The new make spirit is aged in wooden casks, often oak barrels. During this time, the whiskey develops its flavors, colors, and complexities.

5. Bottling: After aging for a predetermined period, the whiskey is filtered and diluted to the desired alcohol content before being bottled and sold.

Understanding the different types of whiskey and the distillation process is just the beginning of your journey into the world of whiskey-making. In the following chapters, we will delve deeper into the intricacies of creating your own distinct whiskey and turning it into a successful business. So, raise your glass to the knowledge you've gained in this chapter, for it is the foundation upon which your whiskey dreams will be built.

Chapter 3
Market Research

Navigating the Whiskey Landscape

Before you dive headfirst into starting your whiskey business, it's essential to navigate the whiskey landscape through thorough market research. Understanding your potential consumers, the competition, and the market dynamics is the key to making informed decisions. In this chapter, we will explore the ins and outs of conducting effective market research for your whiskey venture.

Identifying Your Target Audience

Understanding your target audience is the cornerstone of any successful business. In the world of whiskey, your target audience might be as diverse as the flavors and aromas in a well-aged single malt. Here are some key points to consider:

1. Demographics: Analyze the age, gender, income level, and location of your potential customers. Whiskey enthusiasts come from various backgrounds.

2. Preferences: Determine the styles and types of whiskey that your target audience prefers. Do they lean towards bourbon, Scotch, or something else?

3. Occasions: Identify the occasions when your whiskey is likely to be consumed. Is it a celebratory drink, a choice for special events, or a daily indulgence?

4. Price Sensitivity: Understand how price-sensitive your target audience is. This will influence your pricing strategy.

5. Lifestyle and Values: Consider the values and lifestyle choices of your audience. Some may appreciate locally sourced and sustainable products, while others may be connoisseurs seeking rare and aged whiskeys.

Analyzing the Competition

In the world of whiskey, competition is fierce. Recognizing your competitors and what sets you apart is essential. Here's how to analyze the competition effectively:

1. Competitor Assessment: List your competitors, both locally and nationally or internationally. Study their products, pricing, and marketing strategies.

2. Unique Selling Proposition (USP): Identify your USP – what makes your whiskey stand out? It could be the ingredients, the distillation process, or the brand story.

3. Gaps in the Market: Look for opportunities or gaps in the market that your whiskey can fill. Is there a specific niche not addressed by existing brands?

4. Pricing Strategy: Understand how your competitors price their products. Determine where your whiskey fits in terms of price and value.

5. Marketing and Branding: Analyze the marketing efforts and branding of competitors. What can you do differently to capture consumer attention?

Market Trends and Dynamics

To succeed in the whiskey business, you need to be aware of current market trends and dynamics. Some aspects to consider include:

1. Craft Whiskey Boom: The craft distillery movement is gaining momentum. Consumers often seek unique and small-batch whiskeys.

2. Flavored Whiskeys: The market has seen a rise in flavored whiskeys, appealing to those who enjoy more diverse taste profiles.

3. Sustainability: Environmental and ethical concerns are influencing consumer choices. Implementing sustainable practices can be a competitive advantage.

4. Online and E-commerce: The growth of online platforms and e-commerce is changing how whiskey is distributed and sold.

5. Regulatory Changes: Stay informed about any changes in regulations that may affect your business, including tax laws and labeling requirements.

Effective market research will be your compass as you navigate the whiskey landscape. It will help you make informed decisions, tailor your products to your target audience, and position your whiskey business for success. In the following chapters, we will delve into the practical aspects of turning your market research into a solid business plan. Cheers to your journey into the world of whiskey entrepreneurship!

Chapter 4
Business Planning

The Blueprint for Your Whiskey Venture

In the world of whiskey entrepreneurship, a well-crafted business plan is your roadmap to success. It's not just a document; it's the blueprint for your venture, outlining your goals, strategies, and the steps you need to take to turn your whiskey dreams into reality. In this chapter, we'll explore the essential components of a whiskey business plan and how to create one that sets you on the path to success.

The Importance of a Business Plan

A business plan is your strategic guide. It serves multiple crucial purposes, such as:

1. Setting Clear Objectives: It defines your business's goals and what you aim to achieve.

2. Attracting Investors: A well-structured business plan can help you secure funding and partnerships.

3. Decision-Making Tool: It provides a framework for making informed decisions as your business evolves.

4. Communication Tool: Your plan can be shared with team members, potential employees, and other stakeholders to convey your vision and strategy.

5. Risk Management: It helps you anticipate challenges and plan for contingencies.

Key Components of a Whiskey Business Plan

1. Executive Summary: This is a concise overview of your entire business plan, including the most critical aspects of your venture.

2. Business Description: Provide a detailed description of your whiskey business, including your mission, vision, and unique selling proposition (USP).

3. Market Research: Include the results of your market research, highlighting your target audience, competition, and market trends.

4. Product Line: Describe the types of whiskey you plan to produce, their characteristics, and any special features.

5. Marketing and Sales Strategy: Outline how you intend to market and sell your whiskey. Include pricing, distribution, and promotion strategies.

6. Operational Plan: Detail the day-to-day operations of your distillery, including production, quality control, and staffing requirements.

7. Financial Projections: Provide financial forecasts, including income statements, balance sheets, and cash flow projections. Investors will scrutinize this section.

8. Funding Needs: Specify how much capital you require to launch and operate your whiskey business. Explain how you'll use the funds.

9. Legal and Regulatory Compliance: Describe the licenses, permits, and regulatory requirements necessary for your distillery.

10. Risk Analysis: Identify potential risks and challenges your business may face and propose strategies for mitigating them.

Writing Your Business Plan

Creating a whiskey business plan is a detailed process that requires research, thought, and careful consideration. Here are some steps to help you get started:

1. Research and Data Collection: Gather all the information you need to support the components of your plan, including market research and financial data.

2. Outline Your Plan: Begin by creating an outline that details what each section will cover.

3. Write Your Plan: Start filling in the details for each section, ensuring that your plan is well-organized and concise.

4. Seek Professional Advice: Consider consulting with experts, such as accountants, lawyers, or industry veterans, to ensure your plan is sound.

5. Review and Revise: Regularly review and revise your business plan to adapt to changing circumstances and goals.

6. Prepare for Presentations: Be ready to present your plan to potential investors or partners with confidence and clarity.

Your business plan is a living document that should evolve as your whiskey business grows. It's not set in stone but should be a flexible tool that guides your decisions and strategies. In the following chapters, we will delve into the practical aspects of bringing your whiskey business to life, from legal considerations to setting up your distillery.

Chapter 5
Legal Considerations

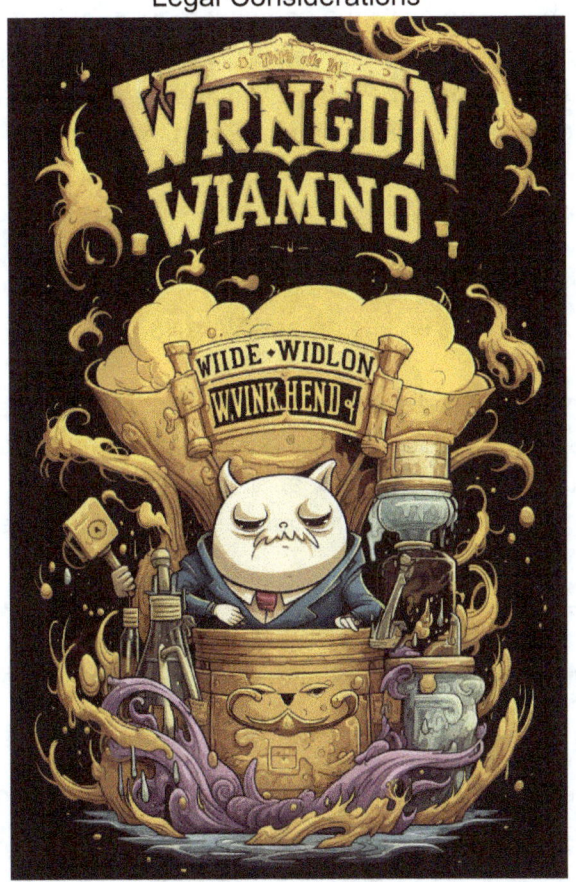

Navigating the Regulatory Landscape of Whiskey

Starting a whiskey business is a dream come true for many, but it comes with a complex regulatory landscape that you must navigate. The production, distribution, and sale of alcoholic beverages, including whiskey, are subject to various local, national, and international laws. In this chapter, we'll explore the critical legal considerations you need to address to operate your whiskey business within the bounds of the law.

Licensing and Permits

One of the first steps in establishing your whiskey business is obtaining the necessary licenses and permits. These vary by location and the type of alcohol you intend to produce, but they typically include:

1. Distillery License: This is the primary license that allows you to produce whiskey. It's issued by government authorities and often involves extensive background checks and inspections.

2. Federal Alcohol Permit: In the United States, you'll need to secure a Federal Distilled Spirits Plant (DSP) permit from the Alcohol and Tobacco Tax and Trade Bureau (TTB).

3. State and Local Licenses: Many regions require additional licenses at the state and local levels, including state alcohol permits, health permits, and business licenses.

4. Sales and Distribution Licenses: If you plan to sell your whiskey directly to consumers or through retail outlets, you may need specific sales and distribution licenses.

5. Export Licenses: If you intend to export your whiskey internationally, you'll need the appropriate export permits and comply with the regulations of the destination country.

Compliance with Regulations

Ensuring compliance with regulations is an ongoing and critical aspect of running a whiskey business. Here are some important areas to consider:

1. Labeling and Brand Approval: The labels on your whiskey bottles must adhere to strict regulations, including accurate proof, origin, and health warning statements.

2. Quality and Safety Standards: Maintaining the quality and safety of your whiskey is paramount. Compliance with quality standards ensures consumer safety and satisfaction.

3. Record-Keeping: Whiskey producers are typically required to maintain meticulous records of production, inventory, and sales for inspection.

4. Taxation: Alcoholic beverages are heavily taxed in many countries. You must understand the tax regulations and ensure proper tax reporting and payment.

5. Advertising and Promotion: Regulations often govern how you can advertise and promote alcoholic beverages. This includes restrictions on marketing to minors and responsible drinking messages.

6. Environmental Regulations: Depending on your distillery's location and size, you may need to comply with environmental regulations related to water use, waste disposal, and emissions.

Responsibility and Accountability

Operating a whiskey business requires a strong sense of responsibility and accountability. Here are some ways to ensure you maintain high standards of legality and ethics:

1. Stay Informed: Keep yourself updated on changes in alcohol-related laws and regulations at the local, national, and international levels.

2. Hire Legal Counsel: It's wise to have legal counsel or a compliance expert on your team to ensure you're always in compliance with the law.

3. Training and Education: Ensure your staff is well-trained in alcohol laws and responsible service of alcohol to prevent legal violations.

4. Community Engagement: Building positive relationships with the local community can help smooth the regulatory process and demonstrate your commitment to being a responsible business owner.

Navigating the legal landscape of the whiskey industry can be challenging, but it's essential for the success and longevity of your business. By understanding the licensing and regulatory requirements, adhering to them diligently, and seeking legal advice when necessary, you can operate your whiskey business with confidence and integrity. In the following chapters, we will delve into other key aspects, such as selecting the right location and equipment for your distillery.

Chapter 6

Location and Facilities

Choosing the Right Setting for Your Whiskey Dream

The location of your distillery and the facilities you choose will significantly impact the success of your whiskey business. It's not just a place to make whiskey; it's where your brand comes to life, and it can influence the flavors and character of your spirits. In this chapter, we will explore the considerations for selecting the perfect location and setting up the facilities for your whiskey venture.

Selecting the Ideal Location

1. Accessibility: Consider how accessible your distillery will be for both visitors and suppliers. A convenient location can enhance your business's efficiency and attractiveness to tourists.

2. Proximity to Resources: Being close to the raw materials you need, such as grain and water sources, can reduce transportation costs and benefit your production process.

3. Regulatory Zoning: Ensure that the location you choose is zoned for alcohol production and complies with local zoning laws.

4. Tourism Potential: If you plan to offer tours and tastings to visitors, a location with tourism potential can be a significant revenue generator.

5. Community Support: Engage with the local community and authorities to gain their support and cooperation, which can be valuable during the permitting and regulatory process.

Facility Considerations

1. Distillery Layout: Design a layout that optimizes the workflow, ensuring a logical and efficient process from mashing to bottling.

2. Equipment Selection: Choose the right distillation equipment, fermenters, and storage tanks that suit your production scale and style.

3. Aging Warehouse: If you're producing aged whiskey, you'll need an appropriate aging warehouse with climate control to achieve the desired flavors.

4. Quality Control Lab: Set up a quality control lab to test and monitor the quality of your whiskey at various stages of production.

5. Visitor Center: If you plan to attract tourists, create a welcoming and informative visitor center with tasting areas.

6. Storage and Warehousing: Ensure you have sufficient storage space for raw materials, aging barrels, and finished products.

7. Environmental Considerations: Implement eco-friendly practices and design your facilities to minimize environmental impact.

Safety and Compliance

Compliance with safety and regulatory standards is paramount when setting up your distillery. Consider the following:

1. Fire Safety: Install appropriate fire safety measures, including fire-resistant materials, sprinkler systems, and emergency exits.

2. Permitting and Inspections: Be prepared for regular inspections to ensure that your facilities adhere to safety and regulatory standards.

3. Employee Training: Train your staff in safety procedures to minimize the risk of accidents or mishaps.

4. Environmental Impact: Implement practices to minimize your distillery's environmental footprint, such as wastewater treatment and energy-efficient equipment.

5. Accessibility: Ensure your facilities are accessible to all employees and visitors, complying with disability regulations.

The location and facilities you choose for your whiskey business will be the backdrop to your whiskey-making journey. It's essential to find the right balance between practicality, accessibility, and the unique charm that sets your distillery apart. In the following chapters, we will delve deeper into the equipment, ingredients, and production processes involved in crafting your whiskey.

Chapter 7
Equipment and Ingredients

Tools of the Trade in Whiskey-Making

In the whiskey-making process, the right equipment and quality ingredients are the foundation of creating exceptional spirits. This chapter explores the essential tools of the trade and the key ingredients you'll need to craft your whiskey.

Distillation Equipment

The core of any distillery is its distillation equipment. The type and size of your distillation equipment will depend on the scale of your operation and the style of whiskey you plan to produce. Key components include:

1. Pot Stills: These are traditional copper or stainless steel vessels used for batch distillation. They are ideal for producing flavorful and complex spirits.

2. Column Stills: Continuous column stills are efficient for producing a high-proof and neutral spirit. They are commonly used in the production of grain whiskey.

3. Mash Tun: A vessel for mixing and mashing grains with hot water to convert starches into sugars. Mash tuns come in various sizes and styles.

4. Fermentation Tanks: These vessels are where yeast is added to the mash, allowing fermentation to occur. The choice of material and design can influence flavor.

5. Heat Source: Depending on the equipment, you may use direct-fired or steam-based heating methods for distillation.

Aging Barrels

If you plan to produce aged whiskey, the choice of aging barrels is crucial. The wood and size of the barrels play a significant role in flavor development. Common types include:

1. Oak Barrels: White oak barrels are the most popular choice for aging whiskey. The wood imparts flavors and colors to the spirit.

2. Barrel Size: The size of the barrel affects the aging process. Smaller barrels have more surface area in contact with the whiskey and can accelerate aging.

3. Previous Use: Barrels that previously held other spirits, such as sherry or bourbon, can add unique flavor characteristics to your whiskey.

4. Aging Warehouse: Ensure your aging warehouse maintains stable temperature and humidity conditions to achieve consistent aging results.

Ingredients

1. Grains: The choice of grains, such as barley, corn, rye, and wheat, will determine the flavor and character

of your whiskey. Different grain ratios create various whiskey styles.

2. Water: High-quality water is essential for mashing and diluting the whiskey. Water source and composition can impact the final product.

3. Yeast: Yeast strains influence the fermentation process and the resulting flavor profiles of your whiskey.

4. Adjuncts: Some recipes may include adjuncts like fruits, spices, or herbs to create unique flavor profiles or variations.

5. Wood and Char: If you're aging in new barrels, the wood type and level of char will influence flavor and color.

6. Water Treatment: Depending on your water source, you may need to treat it to ensure it's suitable for whiskey production.

Quality Control

Maintaining consistent quality in your whiskey production is critical. Establish a quality control process that includes regular tasting and chemical analysis to ensure that your whiskey meets your desired flavor profile and safety standards.

Production Efficiency

Optimize the efficiency of your production process by setting up effective workflows, monitoring fermentation, and distillation parameters, and maintaining equipment in good condition.

Sourcing Suppliers

Identify reliable suppliers for grains, barrels, and other essential materials. Establish strong relationships to ensure a consistent supply chain.

The equipment you choose and the ingredients you use are the tools that enable you to create whiskey with its own unique character and identity. As you embark on your whiskey-making journey, your choices in equipment and ingredients will be instrumental in crafting the flavors that will make your whiskey stand out. In the upcoming chapters, we'll dive into the step-by-step whiskey production process and explore the art and science of creating your signature spirits.

Chapter 8
Production Process

The Alchemy of Whiskey-Making

The heart and soul of your whiskey business lie in the production process. This chapter will take you on a journey through the alchemy of whiskey-making, from the initial mashing of grains to the final bottling and labeling of your spirits. Understanding each step is essential to crafting high-quality, distinctive whiskeys.

1. Mashing and Fermentation

Mashing: The whiskey-making process begins with mashing, where you combine grains, usually a blend of barley, corn, rye, or wheat, with hot water. The purpose is to convert the starches in the grains into fermentable sugars. The result is a sugary liquid known as "wort."

Fermentation: After mashing, yeast is added to the wort to initiate fermentation. The yeast consumes the sugars and produces alcohol and carbon dioxide. This stage can last several days, and the result is a liquid called "wash" with low alcohol content.

2. Distillation

Distillation: The wash is heated in a still to separate alcohol from water and other compounds. The distillation process typically involves two rounds: the wash is first distilled in a wash still, and then the resulting liquid, known as "low wines," is distilled again in a spirit still. This double distillation process increases the alcohol content.

Heads, Hearts, and Tails: During distillation, the distillate is divided into "heads," "hearts," and "tails." The "hearts" are the desirable middle portion with the highest-quality alcohol and flavor. The "heads" and "tails" contain undesirable compounds and are often re-distilled or discarded.

3. Aging in Barrels

Aging: If you plan to produce aged whiskey, the next step is to transfer the new make spirit into oak barrels. The aging process allows the whiskey to develop its unique flavors, aromas, and colors. The type of wood, barrel size, and aging conditions all play a role in the final product.

4. Blending and Dilution

Blending: For some whiskey styles, blending is a critical step. It involves mixing different whiskeys to achieve a consistent flavor profile.

Dilution: Before bottling, the whiskey may be diluted with water to reach the desired alcohol content. This is often done with precision to achieve the target proof.

5. Bottling and Labeling

Bottling: The final whiskey is filtered, often to remove any remaining solids, and then carefully bottled. The choice of bottle and closure is part of your brand's identity.

Labeling: Labels must meet regulatory requirements and include essential information, such as the whiskey's name, alcohol content, and origin. This is an opportunity to tell your brand's story.

Quality Control and Consistency

Quality control is a continuous process throughout the production journey. It involves regular tasting, chemical analysis, and sensory evaluation to ensure that each batch meets your desired flavor profile and safety standards. Consistency is vital in the world of whiskey, and your customers will come to expect a particular flavor and quality from your brand.

A Masterful Balancing Act

Whiskey-making is a combination of art and science, where each step influences the final product. The choice of grains, the distillation process, and the aging conditions are all elements you can experiment with to create a whiskey that reflects your vision and style.

In the following chapters, we will explore the nuances of branding and marketing, distribution and sales strategies, financial management, and other key elements to help you succeed in the world of whiskey entrepreneurship. Your journey is akin to that of a master distiller, where precision, passion, and artistry come together to create liquid gold.

Chapter 9
Branding and Marketing

Crafting Your Whiskey Identity

In the competitive world of whiskey, your brand's identity is as important as the quality of your spirits. This chapter explores the art of branding and the strategies you can employ to market your whiskey effectively, connect with your audience, and differentiate your business in a crowded marketplace.

Understanding Branding

1. Brand Identity: Your brand identity is the essence of your whiskey business. It encompasses your company's name, logo, packaging, and the values you stand for. Consider what your brand will represent and how it will resonate with your target audience.

2. Storytelling: Craft a compelling brand story that tells the narrative of your whiskey journey. Share your passion, history, and the unique aspects of your brand. A well-told story can engage customers and create an emotional connection.

3. Visual Branding: Your logo and label design should be visually appealing and reflect the essence of your brand. The label is often the first point of contact with consumers, so it should stand out on the shelf.

Effective Marketing Strategies

1. Online Presence: In today's digital age, having a strong online presence is essential. Create a

professional website and engage with your audience on social media platforms. Share the behind-the-scenes process, stories, and updates about your whiskey brand.

2. Content Marketing: Produce high-quality content that educates, entertains, and informs your audience about whiskey. Blogs, videos, and social media posts can be used to share your knowledge and passion.

3. Whiskey Tastings and Events: Hosting tastings and events at your distillery or partnering with bars and restaurants for whiskey events can introduce your brand to a wider audience.

4. Collaborations: Partner with other businesses, distilleries, or restaurants to create unique collaborations and limited-edition releases. These partnerships can be mutually beneficial and generate excitement.

5. Whiskey Tours: Offer distillery tours and tastings to educate visitors about the whiskey-making process and immerse them in your brand's story.

6. Awards and Recognition: Participate in whiskey competitions and awards to gain recognition for your products. Winning awards can boost your brand's credibility and reputation.

Distribution and Sales Strategies

1. Distribution Channels: Choose the right distribution channels for your whiskey, whether it's through retailers, bars, restaurants, or online sales. Consider factors like reach, cost, and control.

2. Pricing Strategy: Set competitive and appropriate pricing that reflects the quality and uniqueness of your whiskey. Pricing can influence consumer perception and demand.

3. Sales Team: If you have a sales team, ensure they are well-trained and knowledgeable about your products. Their enthusiasm and expertise can influence buyers' decisions.

4. Customer Engagement: Develop strategies to engage with your customers directly. Collect feedback, respond to inquiries, and create loyalty programs to build a dedicated customer base.

Legal Compliance in Marketing

Ensure your marketing efforts are compliant with local and international laws and regulations, especially those pertaining to alcohol advertising. Avoid marketing to underage audiences, make responsible drinking messages part of your campaigns, and adhere to labeling requirements.

Your brand's identity and marketing strategies are essential components of building a successful whiskey business. By understanding your target audience, crafting a compelling brand story, and implementing effective marketing and distribution plans, you can connect with consumers, build loyalty, and make your mark in the world of whiskey. In the following chapters, we'll explore distribution and sales, financial management, and other aspects of running a thriving whiskey venture.

Chapter 10
Distribution and Sales

Getting Your Whiskey into the Hands of Enthusiasts

Distribution and sales are crucial aspects of running a successful whiskey business. While producing an exceptional product is vital, getting it into the hands of consumers is equally important. In this chapter, we will explore the intricacies of distribution and sales strategies for your whiskey venture.

Choosing the Right Distribution Model

1. Three-Tier System: In some regions, a three-tier distribution system is mandatory, where producers must sell to distributors who, in turn, sell to retailers. Understanding and adhering to this system is essential.

2. Direct-to-Consumer (DTC): Some distilleries sell their products directly to consumers through their own tasting rooms, websites, or clubs. DTC sales can be profitable and provide a direct connection with your customers.

3. Wholesalers and Distributors: If you choose to work with wholesalers or distributors, carefully select partners who align with your brand and have the reach and resources to expand your distribution.

Effective Sales Strategies

1. Sales Team: If you have a sales team, ensure they are well-trained, passionate, and knowledgeable about your whiskey. They are your brand ambassadors and

play a crucial role in building relationships with retailers and bars.

2. Merchandising: Work with retailers and bars to create appealing displays and promotions that attract consumers to your products. Eye-catching merchandising can boost sales.

3. Brand Ambassadors: Appoint brand ambassadors who can conduct tastings and educate consumers about your whiskey. Personal connections can drive sales and loyalty.

4. Trade Shows and Events: Participate in industry events, trade shows, and whiskey festivals to showcase your products, network, and gain exposure to potential distributors, retailers, and customers.

5. Online Sales: In the digital age, consider selling your whiskey through e-commerce platforms. An attractive and user-friendly website can make online sales a significant revenue stream.

Pricing and Margins

Setting the right pricing strategy is a delicate balance. Consider factors like production costs, distribution costs, and the perceived value of your whiskey. Ensure that your pricing allows for competitive margins while keeping your product accessible to your target audience.

Regulatory Compliance

Navigating the legal and regulatory landscape is crucial in distribution and sales:

1. Alcohol Laws: Stay informed about alcohol laws and regulations that govern the sale and distribution of alcoholic beverages in your region.

2. Labeling and Packaging: Ensure that your labels and packaging meet the legal requirements for your whiskey.

3. Taxation: Comply with tax laws related to the sale of alcoholic beverages. Understand excise taxes and how they apply to your products.

Marketing and Promotion

Promote your whiskey through various channels:

1. Advertising: Consider advertising in whiskey publications, on social media, and through partnerships to reach your target audience.

2. Brand Events: Host brand events and whiskey tastings to engage with consumers and promote your products.

3. Social Media: Utilize social media platforms to share your brand's story, connect with enthusiasts, and showcase your products.

4. Collaborations: Collaborate with other businesses, bars, and restaurants to introduce your products to a wider audience.

Effective distribution and sales strategies, combined with a compelling brand story and quality product, can set your whiskey business on a path to success. In the following chapters, we'll delve into financial management, scaling your business, and ensuring the long-term sustainability of your venture in the competitive world of whiskey.

Chapter 11
Financial Management

Nurturing the Financial Health of Your Whiskey Business

Financial management is the backbone of any successful whiskey business. It involves careful planning, tracking, and control of your finances to ensure that your venture remains profitable and sustainable. In this chapter, we will explore the key aspects of financial management for your whiskey business.

1. Budgeting and Financial Planning

Budget Creation: Develop a comprehensive budget that includes your startup costs, ongoing operational expenses, and revenue projections. A well-structured budget will serve as a roadmap for your financial activities.

Cash Flow Management: Monitor your cash flow regularly to ensure that you have sufficient funds to cover your expenses, including raw materials, labor, and overhead costs.

Sales Forecasting: Accurate sales forecasting is essential for budgeting and resource allocation. Consider different scenarios and market trends to make informed predictions.

2. Funding Your Whiskey Business

Initial Capital: Determine how you will finance your whiskey business, whether through personal savings, loans, investors, or crowdfunding. Carefully assess the financial risks and rewards associated with each option.

Working Capital: Maintain an adequate level of working capital to cover day-to-day expenses, such as rent, utilities, and payroll.

Investment in Equipment and Aging: Allocate funds for equipment, aging barrels, and storage facilities, taking into account the upfront costs and long-term benefits.

3. Cost Control and Efficiency

Cost of Goods Sold (COGS): Monitor your COGS, which includes the costs associated with producing your whiskey. Efficient production and ingredient sourcing can help control these costs.

Labor Costs: Manage your labor costs by optimizing staffing and productivity. Consider cross-training employees to handle multiple roles.

Overhead Expenses: Keep an eye on overhead expenses, such as rent, utilities, and administrative costs. Identify areas where cost savings can be achieved.

4. Pricing Strategy

Set pricing that reflects the value and quality of your whiskey. Consider factors such as production costs, competition, and customer demand. A well-balanced pricing strategy can maximize profitability.

5. Financial Reporting and Analysis

Implement a financial reporting system that provides regular insights into your business's financial performance. Key financial reports include income statements, balance sheets, and cash flow statements.

Variance Analysis: Regularly compare your actual financial results to your budgeted figures. Identify discrepancies and take corrective actions when necessary.

KPIs and Metrics: Track key performance indicators (KPIs) specific to the whiskey industry, such as production yield, bottle turnover, and inventory turnover.

6. Taxation and Compliance

Understand the tax obligations related to the production and sale of alcoholic beverages in your region. Comply with excise taxes, sales taxes, and other tax regulations.

Record-Keeping: Maintain meticulous records of financial transactions and tax-related documents to facilitate tax reporting and compliance.

7. Risk Management

Identify potential financial risks that could impact your whiskey business, such as market fluctuations, regulatory changes, and supply chain disruptions. Develop contingency plans to mitigate these risks.

8. Scaling Your Business

If you plan to expand your operations, carefully consider the financial implications and funding requirements. Scaling should be a calculated step to ensure financial stability.

Financial management is an ongoing process that requires vigilance, adaptability, and informed decision-making. By actively monitoring your finances, controlling costs, and making strategic investments, you can nurture the financial health of your whiskey business and set the stage for growth and success. In the following chapters, we'll explore scaling your business, long-term sustainability, and the evolving landscape of the whiskey industry.

Chapter 12
Hiring and Team Building

Building the Right Team for Your Whiskey Business

Your whiskey business's success isn't solely determined by the quality of your product; it also relies on the quality of the team behind it. In this chapter, we'll explore the key aspects of hiring and team building, helping you assemble a team that's passionate, skilled, and aligned with your vision.

1. Define Your Team Needs

Before you start hiring, it's essential to define the roles and positions you need within your whiskey business. Consider the following:

- Distillery Staff: This includes distillers, cellar workers, and other production roles.
- Sales and Marketing Team: Responsible for promoting and distributing your whiskey.
- Administrative and Support Roles: For tasks like accounting, compliance, and customer service.
- Management and Leadership: Including roles like a distillery manager or operations director.

2. Attracting Talent

Attracting the right talent is crucial. Consider the following strategies:

- Employer Branding: Build an attractive employer brand by showcasing your company culture, values, and commitment to quality.

- Networking: Attend industry events and network to connect with potential hires.
- Job Listings: Use online job boards, your website, and social media to post job openings.
- Referrals: Encourage employee referrals, as they often lead to quality candidates who fit your team culture.

3. Hiring Process

A well-structured hiring process ensures you select candidates who align with your vision and values. The process typically includes:

- Application and Resume Review: Screen applicants based on their qualifications and experience.
- Interviews: Conduct structured interviews to assess skills, culture fit, and passion for your business.
- Skills Assessment: For production roles, consider practical skills assessments.
- Background Checks: Ensure candidates have a clean record.
- References: Contact previous employers or colleagues for insights into a candidate's work ethic and character.

4. Onboarding and Training

Once you've selected the right candidates, effective onboarding and training are essential. This involves:

- Orientation: Introduce new hires to your distillery, its culture, and your products.

- Training: Provide job-specific training to ensure they are skilled and knowledgeable in their roles.
- Mentoring: Assign mentors or trainers to help new employees acclimate to their positions.

5. Team Culture and Morale

Creating a positive team culture is essential for long-term success. Consider:

- Communication: Encourage open and transparent communication among team members.
- Recognition: Acknowledge and celebrate achievements to boost morale.
- Feedback: Regularly solicit feedback from your team to address concerns and foster continuous improvement.
- Team-Building Activities: Plan team-building events to strengthen relationships and morale.

6. Retention Strategies

Retaining talented employees is as important as hiring them. Consider:

- Competitive Compensation: Offer competitive salaries and benefits to attract and retain top talent.
- Professional Development: Invest in ongoing training and development opportunities.
- Career Advancement: Provide a clear path for career advancement within your business.

- Recognition and Rewards: Acknowledge and reward outstanding performance.

7. Adapting to Challenges

Address team challenges proactively, whether they're related to interpersonal conflicts, work dynamics, or external factors like industry changes. An adaptable team can navigate challenges more effectively.

8. Legal and Compliance Considerations

Understand and comply with labor laws and regulations in your region. This includes employment contracts, minimum wage, working hours, and workplace safety.

Hiring and team building are ongoing processes. Continuously assess your team's needs, attract and retain top talent, and foster a supportive and engaging team culture. The right team can make all the difference in your whiskey business's success, ensuring that your vision and passion are translated into exceptional products and memorable customer experiences.

Chapter 13
Sustainability in Whiskey Production

Crafting Whiskey with Care for the Environment

Sustainability has become an essential consideration in the whiskey industry as consumers and distilleries alike recognize the need to minimize the environmental impact of production. This chapter explores the concept of sustainability in whiskey production and provides practical guidance on integrating sustainable practices into your distillery.

Understanding Sustainability

Sustainability in whiskey production involves adopting practices that prioritize the long-term well-being of the environment, society, and the distillery itself. It aims to reduce waste, conserve resources, and minimize the environmental footprint while maintaining the integrity of the product and its production process.

Sustainable Practices in Whiskey Production

1. Water Management:

- Source Water Conservation: Be mindful of the water source you use for production. Minimize water wastage and consider using rainwater harvesting or recycling wastewater.
- Efficient Cooling Systems: Opt for water-saving cooling systems to reduce water consumption in the distillation process.

2. Energy Efficiency:

- Use Renewable Energy: Explore the use of renewable energy sources like solar or wind power to reduce reliance on fossil fuels.
- Energy-efficient Equipment: Invest in energy-efficient distillation equipment to minimize energy consumption.

3. Raw Material Sourcing:

- Sustainable Agriculture: Encourage local and sustainable agricultural practices for sourcing grains and other ingredients.
- Ethical Sourcing: Ensure that your raw material suppliers adhere to ethical and sustainable standards.

4. Waste Reduction and Management:

- Recycling: Implement a robust recycling program for materials like glass bottles and packaging.
- Byproduct Utilization: Find creative uses for byproducts of the distillation process, such as using spent grains for animal feed or energy production.

5. Packaging and Design:

- Eco-friendly Packaging: Opt for environmentally friendly packaging materials and designs, such as recycled or recyclable materials.
- Lightweight Glass: Consider lightweight glass bottles to reduce transportation and production energy.

6. Transportation and Distribution:

- Local Sourcing: Whenever possible, source raw materials and distribute products locally to minimize carbon emissions from transportation.
- Efficient Transportation: Optimize transportation routes and methods to reduce energy consumption.

7. Community Engagement:

- Community Partnerships: Engage with local communities and support sustainability initiatives in the areas where your distillery operates.

8. Regulatory Compliance:

- Environmental Regulations: Stay informed about and adhere to environmental regulations that govern whiskey production, waste disposal, and water usage.

Sustainable Certification and Labels

Consider seeking certifications like "organic," "sustainable," or "green" for your whiskey products. These labels can communicate your commitment to sustainable practices to consumers and may attract environmentally conscious buyers.

Educate and Engage

Educate your team and engage them in sustainability efforts. Encourage them to come up with ideas for reducing waste and conserving resources.

Consumer Awareness

Share your sustainability efforts with consumers. Transparent communication can create a positive brand image and resonate with environmentally conscious consumers.

Measuring and Reporting

Establish a system for measuring and reporting on sustainability metrics. This data can guide your sustainability efforts and demonstrate your commitment to stakeholders.

Sustainability in whiskey production is not just a trend but a long-term commitment to preserving the environment and resources for future generations. By integrating sustainable practices into your distillery, you can not only reduce your environmental impact but also enhance your brand's reputation and appeal to consumers who prioritize sustainability in their purchasing decisions.

Chapter 14
Building Partnerships in the Whiskey Business

Collaboration and Alliances for Success

The whiskey industry is a tight-knit community, and building partnerships can be a strategic way to grow your business, expand your reach, and create unique opportunities. In this chapter, we'll explore the art of building partnerships in the whiskey business.

Understanding the Value of Partnerships

Partnerships in the whiskey industry can take various forms and offer numerous benefits:

1. Access to Resources: Partnerships can provide access to resources, whether it's raw materials, distribution networks, or knowledge and expertise.

2. Mutual Promotion: Collaborations often involve mutual promotion, allowing both partners to reach new audiences and build brand awareness.

3. Innovation: Partnering with other distilleries or businesses can lead to innovation and the creation of unique products, limited editions, or special releases.

4. Market Expansion: Partnerships can open doors to new markets, both locally and internationally.

5. Shared Costs: Collaborating on marketing campaigns, events, or product development can reduce costs and increase efficiency.

Types of Partnerships

1. Distillery Collaborations: Collaborate with other distilleries to create unique blends or limited-edition products. Joint releases can generate excitement among enthusiasts.

2. Supplier Partnerships: Forge strong relationships with suppliers for raw materials, barrels, and other key components. Reliable suppliers are essential for quality production.

3. Distributor Alliances: Build alliances with distributors to expand your distribution network. Joint marketing efforts can help increase sales.

4. Retailer Partnerships: Partner with retailers for exclusive releases or promotions. These partnerships can create a buzz around your products.

5. Bar and Restaurant Collaborations: Work with bars and restaurants to feature your products on their menus or host events. This can introduce your whiskey to a broader audience.

6. Industry Events and Festivals: Participate in whiskey events and festivals to showcase your products and network with other professionals in the industry.

Strategies for Successful Partnerships

1. Clear Objectives: Define your objectives and what you hope to achieve with each partnership. This clarity will guide your efforts.

2. Compatibility: Choose partners who align with your brand values, quality standards, and target audience.

3. Legal Agreements: Create formal agreements that outline the terms and responsibilities of each party. These agreements should cover aspects like product ownership, marketing, and distribution.

4. Effective Communication: Maintain open and transparent communication with your partners. Regularly discuss progress and address any issues promptly.

5. Mutual Benefits: Ensure that the partnership offers benefits to all parties involved. The collaboration should be a win-win situation.

6. Flexibility: Be open to adapting your partnership strategies as the needs of your business and the industry evolve.

Case Studies

Look at successful partnership examples within the whiskey industry for inspiration. Learning from the experiences of others can provide valuable insights.

Networking and Relationship Building

Attend industry events, join associations, and actively engage in the whiskey community to build relationships that can lead to potential partnerships.

Documenting Success

Keep records of successful partnerships, including the strategies, outcomes, and lessons learned. This documentation can guide future efforts.

Building partnerships in the whiskey business can be a dynamic and rewarding process. Collaborations and alliances can lead to new opportunities, innovative products, and increased brand visibility. By approaching partnerships strategically and with a focus on mutual benefits, you can leverage these relationships to elevate your whiskey business to new heights.

Chapter 15

Tasting and Quality Assurance in Whiskey Production

The Pursuit of Perfection

Tasting and quality assurance are the cornerstones of a successful whiskey business. In this chapter, we'll explore the critical role that tasting and quality control play in producing exceptional whiskey.

The Importance of Tasting

Tasting is more than just sipping whiskey; it's an art and a science that involves evaluating a spirit's aroma, flavor, balance, and overall character. Here's why tasting is vital:

1. Quality Benchmark: Tasting is the ultimate quality control tool. It allows you to ensure that each batch meets your standards and delivers the desired flavor profile.

2. Product Consistency: Consistent tasting and quality assessment are essential for maintaining the same flavor and aroma across all your batches.

3. Product Development: Tasting is the foundation of developing new whiskey styles, limited editions, and experimental releases.

4. Consumer Satisfaction: The taste of your whiskey is what consumers will remember and judge your brand by. Exceptional tasting experiences lead to customer loyalty.

Quality Assurance Process

Establishing a robust quality assurance process is crucial for delivering consistent, high-quality whiskey. Here are the key components:

1. Tasting Panels: Form tasting panels with experienced individuals who can assess your whiskey objectively. Panels may include distillers, master blenders, and sensory experts.

2. Sensory Evaluation: Train your team to conduct sensory evaluations, focusing on aroma, flavor, mouthfeel, and finish.

3. Objective Criteria: Develop objective criteria and rating systems to standardize the evaluation process. This helps eliminate subjectivity.

4. Consistency Testing: Conduct regular tasting sessions to evaluate consistency across batches. Any variations should be identified and addressed.

5. Record Keeping: Maintain detailed records of tasting sessions, including notes on each batch's characteristics, any anomalies, and the actions taken to address issues.

6. External Testing: Consider sending samples to external labs for chemical analysis and confirmation of product quality.

Tasting Etiquette

When conducting tastings, adhere to professional etiquette:

1. Clean Palate: Ensure tasters have a clean palate, free from strong odors or tastes.

2. Neutral Environment: Provide a neutral environment free from distractions and strong scents.

3. Proper Glassware: Use appropriate glassware to enhance the tasting experience.

4. Structured Tasting: Follow a structured tasting process that includes evaluating the whiskey's appearance, nose, palate, and finish.

5. Discussion: Encourage open discussion among tasters to capture a range of opinions and insights.

Addressing Quality Issues

If a quality issue arises during a tasting, take the following steps:

1. Identify the Issue: Pinpoint the specific aspect of the whiskey that requires attention. Is it the aroma, flavor, consistency, or any other attribute?

2. Root Cause Analysis: Investigate the root cause of the issue. Was it a one-time anomaly, a process flaw, or an ingredient problem?

3. Corrective Actions: Implement corrective actions to address the issue. This may involve changing the production process, sourcing different ingredients, or refining the aging conditions.

4. Re-Tasting: After making changes, re-taste the whiskey to ensure the issue has been resolved.

Continuous Improvement

Quality assurance is an ongoing process. Continuously seek ways to improve your whiskey production and maintain the highest standards of quality. Regularly update your tasting criteria and involve your team in this journey of continuous improvement.

Tasting and quality assurance are not just about ensuring the quality of your product; they're about delivering memorable tasting experiences to your customers. By focusing on consistent, exceptional quality and creating unique flavor profiles, you can set your whiskey brand apart in a competitive market.

Chapter 16
Crafting an Exceptional Customer Experience in Whiskey Business

From Barrel to Glass, the Journey of Customer Satisfaction

In the whiskey business, customer experience is paramount. This chapter explores the importance of customer experience and provides insights into how you can create exceptional, memorable moments for your customers.

The Significance of Customer Experience

Customer experience encompasses every interaction a customer has with your brand, from the moment they discover your whiskey to the post-purchase support. Here's why it's crucial:

1. Customer Loyalty: A positive experience builds customer loyalty, encouraging repeat purchases and brand advocacy.

2. Brand Reputation: Exceptional experiences foster a strong and positive brand reputation, attracting new customers.

3. Differentiation: In a competitive market, a superior customer experience sets your brand apart and creates a unique selling point.

4. Feedback and Improvement: Engaged customers provide valuable feedback, helping you improve your products and services.

Key Aspects of Customer Experience

1. Brand Identity and Values: Your brand's identity and values should resonate with your target audience, creating a connection that goes beyond the product.

2. Product Quality: Exceptional whiskey quality is the foundation of a memorable experience.

3. Customer Service: Provide responsive and helpful customer service. Address inquiries, concerns, and issues promptly.

4. Educational Content: Share information about your whiskey, distillation process, and history. Educated customers appreciate the product more.

5. Tasting Experiences: Offer tasting sessions and distillery tours that allow customers to engage with your brand and products.

6. Exclusive Releases and Events: Create excitement by offering exclusive releases and hosting events for your loyal customers.

7. Packaging and Presentation: Invest in appealing packaging and presentation, which enhances the overall experience of receiving your product.

8. Transparency: Be transparent about your production process, sourcing, and sustainability efforts. Customers appreciate honesty.

Customizing the Experience

Tailor the customer experience to your audience. Consider different segments of customers and their preferences. For example, enthusiasts may appreciate detailed tasting notes and limited-edition releases, while novices may benefit from educational content and accessible product lines.

Sustainability and Responsibility

Demonstrate environmental and social responsibility in your whiskey production and business practices. Consumers increasingly value brands that are committed to sustainability and responsible drinking.

Feedback and Improvement

Actively seek feedback from your customers and use it to make improvements. Whether it's about product quality, customer service, or other aspects of the experience, customer input is invaluable.

Loyalty Programs and Personalization

Consider implementing loyalty programs and personalization strategies that reward repeat customers and make them feel appreciated.

Community Engagement

Engage with your local and global whiskey communities. Attend industry events, participate in festivals, and foster relationships with enthusiasts and fellow distillers.

Measuring Customer Satisfaction

Use surveys, reviews, and customer satisfaction metrics to assess how well you're meeting customer expectations. Analyze the data and make informed decisions for improvement.

Crafting an exceptional customer experience in the whiskey business goes beyond selling a product; it's about building relationships, fostering loyalty, and creating memorable moments. By focusing on product quality, brand values, educational content, transparency, and personalization, you can make every customer's journey from barrel to glass a delightful and unforgettable one.

Chapter 17
Challenges and Solutions in the Whiskey Business

Navigating the Rocky Road to Success

In the whiskey business, like any entrepreneurial venture, challenges are inevitable. This chapter examines common challenges faced by whiskey entrepreneurs and provides practical solutions to overcome them.

1. Regulatory Challenges

Challenge: Navigating the complex web of alcohol regulations, licensing, and compliance requirements can be daunting and time-consuming.

Solution:
- Consult with legal experts who specialize in alcohol regulations to ensure full compliance.
- Stay updated on changes in regulations that may affect your business.
- Build relationships with local and regional regulatory agencies for smoother interactions.

2. Sourcing Raw Materials

Challenge: Ensuring a consistent and high-quality supply of raw materials, such as grains, can be challenging, especially during market fluctuations.

Solution:
- Establish long-term relationships with reliable suppliers.
- Diversify your supplier base to mitigate risks.

- Consider futures contracts to secure consistent pricing and availability.

3. Competition

Challenge: The whiskey market is competitive, with established brands and new entrants vying for consumer attention.

Solution:
- Differentiate your brand through unique flavors, sustainable practices, and compelling brand storytelling.
- Engage in consumer education and tastings to build brand loyalty.
- Collaborate with other distilleries or businesses to create exclusive offerings that stand out.

4. Quality Control

Challenge: Maintaining consistent product quality across batches can be challenging.

Solution:
- Develop a robust quality assurance program with clear tasting and evaluation criteria.
- Train your team to conduct sensory evaluations and maintain detailed records.
- Regularly taste and assess your whiskey to identify and address quality issues.

5. Financial Management

Challenge: Managing finances, securing capital for expansion, and ensuring profitability can be complex.

Solution:
- Create a detailed financial plan and budget to track expenses and revenues.
- Consider financial management software to streamline bookkeeping.
- Explore funding options such as loans, investors, or grants for expansion.

6. Distribution and Marketing

Challenge: Reaching consumers and gaining shelf space in retail outlets can be a significant hurdle.

Solution:
- Develop a well-defined marketing strategy that includes digital marketing, social media, and brand-building efforts.
- Cultivate relationships with distributors and retailers to expand your distribution network.
- Explore e-commerce as a direct sales channel to reach a broader audience.

7. Sustainability

Challenge: Implementing sustainable practices in production and promoting environmental responsibility can be complex.

Solution:
- Invest in sustainable production methods, like efficient energy use and waste reduction.
- Promote your sustainability efforts through transparent communication with consumers.
- Seek sustainable certifications to validate your commitment to eco-friendly practices.

8. Customer Satisfaction

Challenge: Maintaining a high level of customer satisfaction and managing customer relationships can be demanding.

Solution:
- Invest in customer service and engage with customers promptly and professionally.
- Develop educational content and tasting experiences to enhance customer appreciation of your brand.
- Create loyalty programs and personalize interactions with repeat customers.

9. Expansion and Scaling

Challenge: Scaling your whiskey business while maintaining quality can be a formidable task.

Solution:
- Assess the need for scaling carefully and secure the necessary capital.

- Maintain rigorous quality control measures throughout the scaling process.
- Plan for potential supply chain and production challenges as you expand.

Challenges are an inherent part of running a whiskey business, but with the right strategies and solutions, they can be navigated effectively. By staying informed, building relationships, ensuring consistent quality, and adapting to changing market dynamics, you can overcome obstacles and drive your whiskey business towards success.

Chapter 18
Future Trends in the Whiskey Business

Anticipating and Adapting to Industry Evolution

The whiskey industry is ever-changing, shaped by evolving consumer preferences, technological advances, and environmental concerns. In this chapter, we'll explore the future trends that are likely to impact the whiskey business and how you can position your distillery to thrive in this dynamic landscape.

1. Sustainability Takes Center Stage

Trend: Sustainability will continue to be a dominant theme in the whiskey industry. Consumers increasingly favor brands that prioritize eco-friendly production methods, responsible sourcing, and minimal environmental impact.

Adaptation:
- Invest in sustainable practices, such as energy-efficient distillation equipment, eco-friendly packaging, and waste reduction.
- Communicate your sustainability efforts to consumers, demonstrating your commitment to the environment.

2. Flavored and Innovative Whiskeys

Trend: Distilleries will continue to experiment with flavored and innovative whiskey products, catering to evolving consumer tastes. Flavors like honey, fruit, and botanical infusions are gaining popularity.

Adaptation:

- Explore flavor innovations within your product line to attract a wider audience.
- Stay informed about emerging flavor trends and conduct consumer research to align your offerings.

3. Craft and Artisanal Whiskeys

Trend: Craft and artisanal whiskeys will maintain their appeal, as consumers seek unique, small-batch products with distinctive character and provenance.

Adaptation:
- Embrace your craft identity and continue to focus on quality, storytelling, and limited-edition releases.
- Foster relationships with local communities and enthusiasts who appreciate craft distilling.

4. Online Sales and E-Commerce

Trend: The growth of online sales and e-commerce in the spirits industry will continue. Consumers are increasingly comfortable buying whiskey online.

Adaptation:
- Establish a user-friendly e-commerce platform to sell your products directly to consumers.
- Leverage digital marketing and social media to drive online sales and engagement.

5. Health and Wellness Considerations

Trend: Some consumers are seeking healthier alcohol choices. This trend may lead to the development of low-alcohol, low-calorie, or lower-proof whiskey options.

Adaptation:
- Consider diversifying your product line to include options that align with health and wellness trends.
- Clearly label nutritional information and alcohol content to cater to health-conscious consumers.

6. Whiskey Tourism and Experiences

Trend: Whiskey tourism and distillery experiences are on the rise. Consumers seek immersive visits to distilleries, tastings, and educational opportunities.

Adaptation:
- Develop engaging distillery tours and tasting experiences.
- Invest in visitor centers, tastings, and events that create memorable brand interactions.

7. International Expansion

Trend: International markets will continue to offer growth opportunities for whiskey businesses. Emerging markets in Asia and Latin America are becoming key players in the global whiskey industry.

Adaptation:

- Research and explore the potential of international expansion.
- Adapt your products and marketing strategies to cater to different regions and cultures.

8. Whiskey Technology and Innovation

Trend: Technology will play an increasingly prominent role in whiskey production, from advanced distillation methods to digital marketing and customer engagement.

Adaptation:
- Embrace technology in production for efficiency and quality improvements.
- Stay current with digital marketing trends and utilize online platforms for brand engagement.

Anticipating and adapting to these future trends is essential for the long-term success of your whiskey business. By staying informed, innovating, and aligning your brand with emerging consumer preferences, you can position your distillery to thrive in the dynamic and ever-evolving whiskey industry.

Chapter 19

Expanding Your Whiskey Business

Strategies for Growth and Market Expansion

As your whiskey business evolves and matures, the prospect of expansion becomes an enticing possibility. This chapter explores various strategies for expanding your whiskey business, from broadening your product line to entering new markets and scaling up production.

1. Diversify Your Product Line

Expanding your product line is a practical way to cater to a broader audience and increase sales. Consider the following product diversification strategies:

- Limited Edition Releases: Create limited-edition or seasonal releases to generate excitement and attract collectors and enthusiasts.
- Flavored Whiskeys: Develop flavored whiskey variants, such as honey, fruit-infused, or botanical-flavored expressions, to appeal to diverse tastes.
- Aged and Rare Whiskeys: Invest in longer aging periods to produce aged and rare whiskeys that can command higher prices.
- Whiskey-Based Products: Explore the creation of whiskey-based products like liqueurs, cocktails, or even merchandise that complements your brand.

2. Explore New Markets

Expanding into new markets can significantly boost your customer base and revenue. Consider the following market expansion strategies:

- International Markets: Explore opportunities in international markets, especially emerging regions where whiskey consumption is on the rise.
- Local and Regional Expansion: Consider targeting nearby regions and cities to build a strong local presence and gradually expand your reach.
- Online Sales: Leverage e-commerce to reach a wider audience beyond your immediate geographical area.

3. Scale Up Production

Scaling up production requires careful planning and investment. Here are some strategies for increasing production capacity:

- Invest in Equipment: Upgrade your distillation equipment, aging facilities, and bottling lines to accommodate larger batches.
- Additional Aging Warehouses: Expand your aging capacity by building or acquiring additional warehouses.
- Bulk Sales and Private Labeling: Consider selling bulk whiskey to other distilleries or offering private labeling services for retailers, which can help generate revenue while utilizing your excess capacity

4. Brand Extensions

Extending your brand into related products or services can diversify your revenue streams. Here are some brand extension ideas:

- Merchandise: Create branded merchandise such as glassware, clothing, or accessories.
- Distillery Experiences: Develop distillery tours, tastings, and events to attract visitors and generate additional income.
- Educational Workshops: Offer workshops or courses related to whiskey production, tasting, or mixology.

5. Marketing and Promotion

Expanding your business necessitates increased marketing and promotion efforts. Consider the following marketing strategies:

- Digital Marketing: Invest in digital marketing campaigns, including social media advertising and email marketing, to reach a wider audience.
- Collaborations: Partner with other businesses, influencers, or organizations to promote your brand and expand your reach.
- Public Relations: Engage in public relations efforts to generate media coverage and positive brand recognition.

6. Distribution and Sales Channels

Broaden your distribution and sales channels to increase accessibility to your products. Strategies include:

- Retail Expansion: Secure more shelf space in existing retailers and establish relationships with new ones.
- Direct-to-Consumer Sales: Maximize direct sales to consumers through your distillery, tasting rooms, and e-commerce platforms.
- On-Premises Sales: Explore opportunities to have your products featured in bars, restaurants, and clubs.

7. Strategic Partnerships and Acquisitions

Consider forming strategic partnerships or acquisitions to facilitate expansion. This may involve collaborations with other distilleries, distribution companies, or the acquisition of complementary businesses to expand your portfolio.

8. Innovation and Continuous Improvement

Continuously innovate and improve your products, services, and business processes. This can help you stay competitive and attract new customers.

9. Financial Planning and Investment

Expansion often requires significant financial investment. Create a comprehensive financial plan and explore funding options like loans, grants, investors, or equity financing to support your growth.

10. Market Research and Consumer Insights

Conduct thorough market research and gather consumer insights to guide your expansion strategies. Understanding your target audience and market trends is critical for success.

Expanding your whiskey business is a complex but rewarding endeavor. By carefully planning, executing strategies, and maintaining a strong commitment to quality and customer satisfaction, you can navigate the path to growth and build a thriving, sustainable business.

Chapter 20
Final Thoughts and Takeaways

A Toast to Your Whiskey Journey

As you reach the conclusion of this book on starting and growing a whiskey business, it's time to reflect on the key takeaways and parting advice for your entrepreneurial journey in the world of whiskey.

1. Passion and Dedication

Your passion for whiskey is the driving force behind your business. Stay dedicated to your craft and vision, as this enthusiasm will resonate with consumers and keep you motivated during both challenging and successful times.

2. Quality is Paramount

Quality is non-negotiable in the whiskey industry. Consistently produce high-quality spirits, as this will be the foundation of your brand's reputation and longevity.

3. Storytelling Matters

Craft a compelling brand story that connects with your audience. Share your journey, values, and the essence of your brand to create an emotional connection with consumers.

4. Innovation and Adaptability

Embrace innovation and adaptability. The whiskey industry evolves, and staying relevant requires a willingness to explore new techniques, styles, and marketing strategies.

5. Regulatory Compliance

Compliance with local and international regulations is critical. Be well-informed about legal requirements related to alcohol production, labeling, and distribution in your region.

6. Community Engagement

Build strong relationships with your local community and the broader whiskey community. Engage with other distilleries, enthusiasts, and organizations to create a network that can support your business.

7. Sustainability and Responsibility

Incorporate sustainable practices into your production and demonstrate social responsibility. Aligning your brand with sustainability and responsible drinking can enhance your reputation.

8. Adapt and Grow

Scaling your business and adapting to changing trends is part of the journey. Continuously monitor your market, consumers, and competition, and be ready to pivot when necessary.

9. Legacy and Tradition

Consider the legacy you want to leave in the whiskey industry. Building a lasting tradition involves maintaining quality, preserving traditions, and engaging with the community.

10. Mentorship and Succession

Think about the future of your brand beyond your own involvement. Mentor and groom talent within your business to ensure your legacy endures.

Your journey as a whiskey entrepreneur is a blend of artistry, science, and business acumen. It's a journey marked by passion, persistence, and the pursuit of perfection. As you raise your glass to toast your successes and reflect on the challenges you've overcome, remember that your journey is a remarkable one, and your legacy in the world of whiskey is yours to craft.

May your whiskey business continue to flourish, your brand to thrive, and your legacy to endure for generations to come. Cheers to your success, and may it be as rich and fulfilling as the finest whiskey you produce.